DRINK IT UP!

The Chemistry of Water

Written by William D. Adams

WORLD BOOK

www.worldbook.com

Co-published by agreement between Shi Tu Hui and World Book, Inc.

Shi Tu Hui
Room 1807, Block 1,
#3 West Dawang Road
Chaoyang District, Beijing 100025
P.R. China

World Book, Inc.
180 North LaSalle Street
Suite 900
Chicago, Illinois 60601
USA

© 2026. All rights reserved. This volume may not be reproduced in whole or in part in any form without prior written permission from the publisher.

WORLD BOOK and the GLOBE DEVICE are registered trademarks or trademarks of World Book, Inc.

Library of Congress Control Number: 2025942233

Aha! Academy: Chemistry
ISBN: 978-0-7166-7346-0 (set, hardcover)

Drink It Up! The Chemistry of Water
ISBN: 978-0-7166-7347-7 (hard cover)
ISBN: 978-0-7166-7367-5 (e-book)
ISBN: 978-0-7166-7357-6 (soft cover)

Staff

Editorial

Vice President
Tom Evans

Senior Manager, New Content
Jeff De La Rosa

Senior Curriculum Designer
Caroline Davidson

Curriculum Designer
Mikayla Kightlinger

Content Creator
Joseph P. Cataliotti

Proofreader
Nathalie Strassheim

Indexer
Nathaniel Lindstrom

Graphics and Design

Senior Visual Communications Designer
Melanie Bender

Designer
Shannon Hagman

Written by William D. Adams

Designed by Starletta Polster

Acknowledgments

The publishers gratefully acknowledge the following sources for photography. All illustrations were prepared by WORLD BOOK unless otherwise noted.

Cover: Dmitriy Prayzel/Shutterstock; FotoErkki/Shutterstock; Martin Mecnarowski/Shutterstock; Nature'sLens21/Shutterstock; PeopleImages.com - Yuri A/Shutterstock

© Aaron/Adobe Stock 38, 39; © dam/Adobe Stock 38, 47; © Mona Mäkelä/Adobe Stock 30; © RHJ/Adobe 30; © ronstik/Adobe Stock 5; © Stockfotos/Adobe Stock 3; © sommai/Adobe 30; © tomas/Adobe 39; © Viacheslav Yakobchuk/Adobe 31; © domnitsky/Adobe Stock 30; © fascinadora/Adobe Stock 30, 31; © fotomek/Adobe Stock 6, 7; © logoinspires/Adobe stock 18,14; © Tortuga/Adobe stock 31; © Mary Evans Picture Library/Alamy 9; © ReggieLavoie/iStock 15; © Jean-Yves Glassey & Michel Martinez – Trésor de l'Abbaye de Saint-Maurice/KNF 13; © Jintong Gao and Zhenyuan Xu/MIT 16; © NASA 21; © Gift of Mr. and Mrs. Lawrence Rubin/ Minneapolis Institute of Art 29; Nobel Media (licensed under CC BY 3.0) 23; Public Domain 13; Public Domain (Metropolitan Museum of Art) 18; © Public Health Image Library (PHIL) 33; © Dean Thomas/ROWBOT 36; © Science made alive 26; © Jock Fistick/Reporters/Science Photo Library 27; © Steve Gschmeissner/Science Photo Library 32; © Shutterstock 3, 4, 5, 6, 7, 8, 9, 10, 11, 12, 14, 15, 16, 17, 18, 19, 20, 21, 22, 23, 24, 25, 26, 27, 28, 29, 30, 31, 32, 33, 34, 35, 36, 37, 38, 39, 40, 41, 42, 43, 44, 45, 46, 47, 48; SuSanA Secretariat (licensed under CC BY 2.0) 42, 43; Wellcome Media (licensed under CC BY 4.0) 26

There is a glossary of terms on page 48. Terms defined in the glossary are in type that looks like *this* on their first appearance on any spread (two facing pages).

Contents

Introduction 5

① **The shape of water** 6
- Vital molecule: water 8
- Surface tension 10
- Electrolysis 12
- A soup of ions 14
- Desalination 16
- Water and cleaning 18

② **The elixir of life** 20
- Taking in water 22
- Ocean chemistry 24
- Vital element: chlorine 26

③ **Drinking water** 28
- Tap water taste 30
- Fluoride in tap water 32

④ **Dirty water** 34
- Water damage 36
- Ocean acidification 38
- Wastewater treatment 40
- Treatment alternatives 42

Make a solar still 44

Index 46

Glossary 48

Introduction

Have you had a glass of water lately? If you haven't, you should! Drinking sufficient water helps to keep you healthy, strong, and alert.

Water's importance has made it a vital part of human history. Early human settlements developed around stable water supplies. Modern cities maintain many miles or kilometers of pipes to deliver fresh water to their residents.

Water's not just important for home use—it's also a vital part of manufacturing processes; the main component of weather; and a necessity for all life!

Ever wonder why water is so important? The answer has to do with its chemistry.

1

THE SHAPE OF WATER

Water seems like a basic, elemental substance. What is water made of?

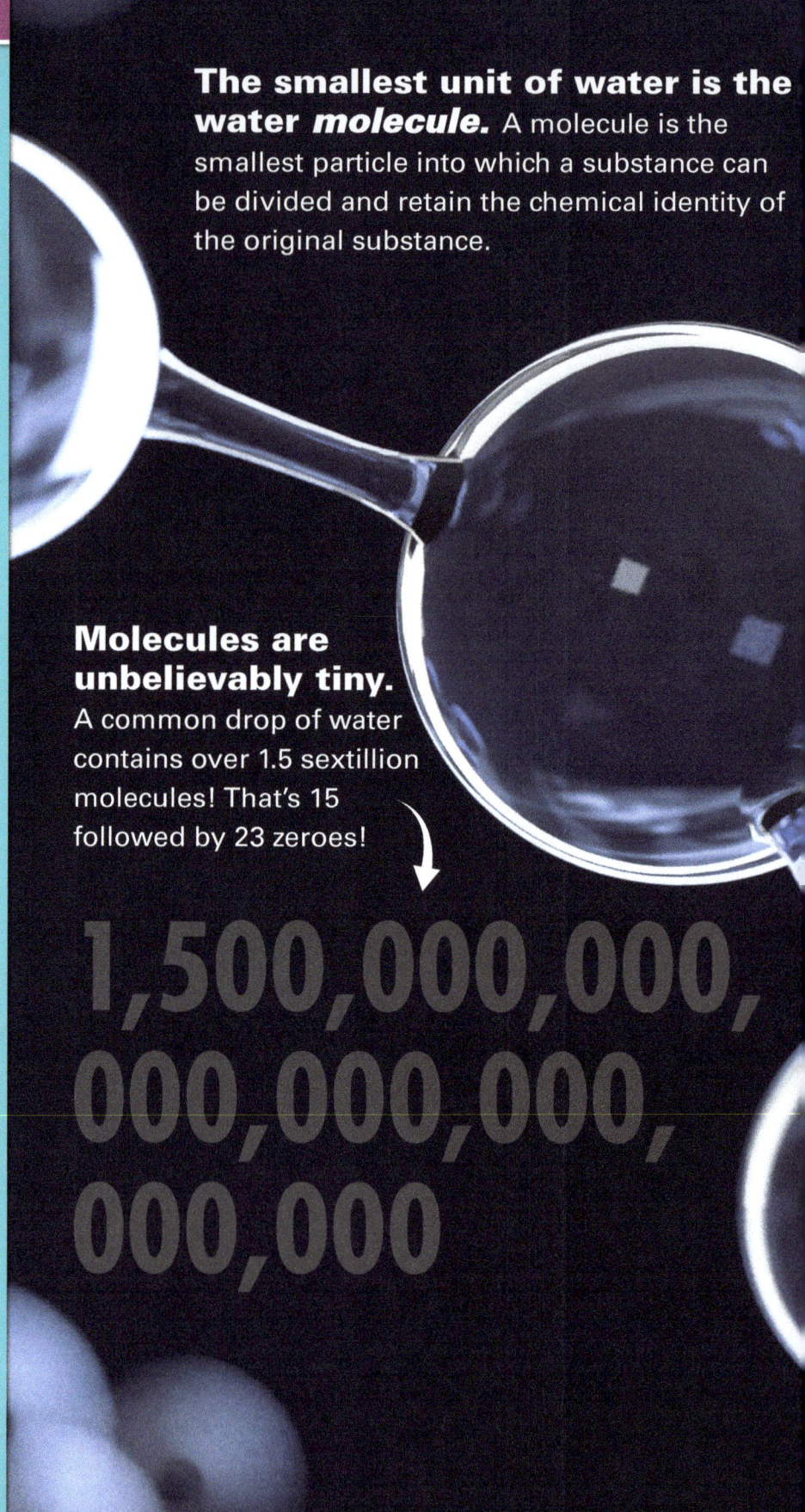

The smallest unit of water is the water *molecule*. A molecule is the smallest particle into which a substance can be divided and retain the chemical identity of the original substance.

Molecules are unbelievably tiny. A common drop of water contains over 1.5 sextillion molecules! That's 15 followed by 23 zeroes!

1,500,000,000,000,000,000,000,000

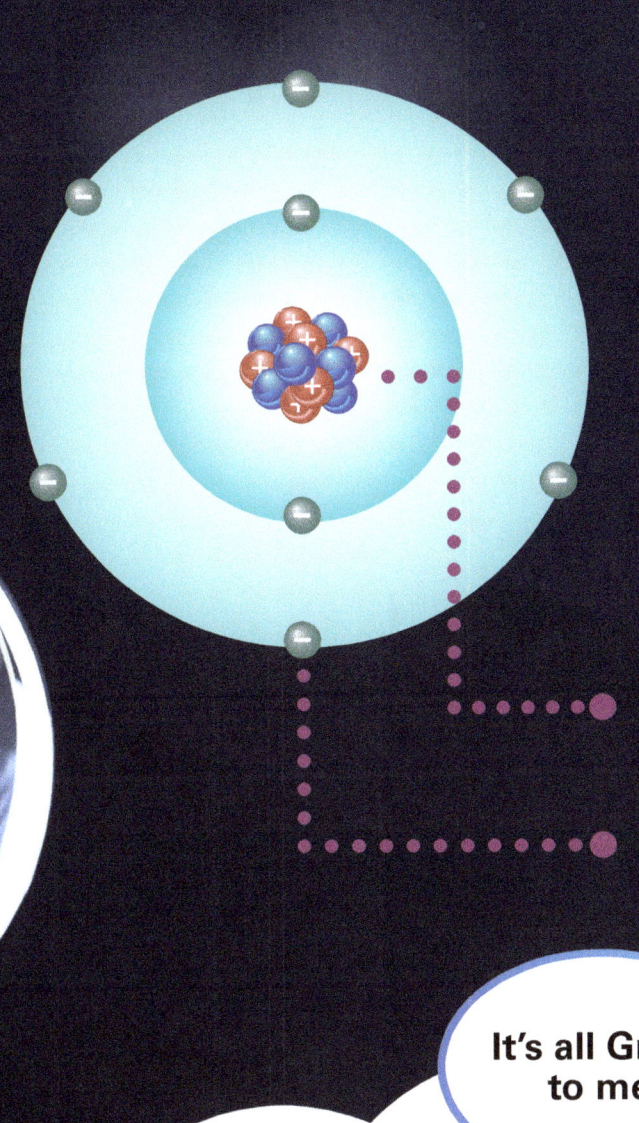

Oxygen atom

- 8 electrons
- 8 protons
- 8 neutrons

Why stop at the molecule?!? Each molecule of water contains two **atoms** of hydrogen and one atom of oxygen. An atom is an even more basic unit of matter. Each atom has a nucleus (core) made of extremely tiny particles called **protons** and **neutrons**.

Even tinier particles called *electrons* move around the nucleus.

It's all Greek to me!

The **ancient Greeks** thought of water as one of the four basic elements, along with earth, wind, and fire. Today, scientists use the word *element* to describe any substance that contains one kind of atom. Scientists have discovered well over a hundred elements, but none of the "classical" elements made the cut.

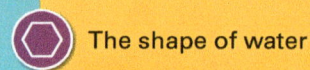

The shape of water

Vital molecule: water

Chemical formula

H_2O

Melting point
32 °F (0 °C)

Boiling point
212 °F (100 °C)

In a water molecule, the two hydrogen *atoms* each share *electrons* with the oxygen atom, forming *covalent bonds.*

The oxygen atom has two sets of unpaired electrons. They repel the electrons in the covalent bonds, pushing them to a 104.45-degree bond angle.

Sometimes, sharing can be unequal! Oxygen attracts the shared electrons more strongly, giving the oxygen side of the molecule a slight negative charge and the hydrogen ends a slight positive charge.

Water's all around us—and even a part of us, but how much do you know about the wet stuff? Here's the scoop on the chemical oxidane—alias, water!

Do the melting and freezing temperatures in Celsius look nice and round? It's no coincidence! Swedish astronomer **Anders Celsius** developed a temperature scale based on the melting and boiling points of water in 1742. However, his original scale labeled water's boiling point as 0 degrees and its freezing point as 100 degrees! Scientists later reversed the scale, but they named it after him just the same.

Brr, it's cold!

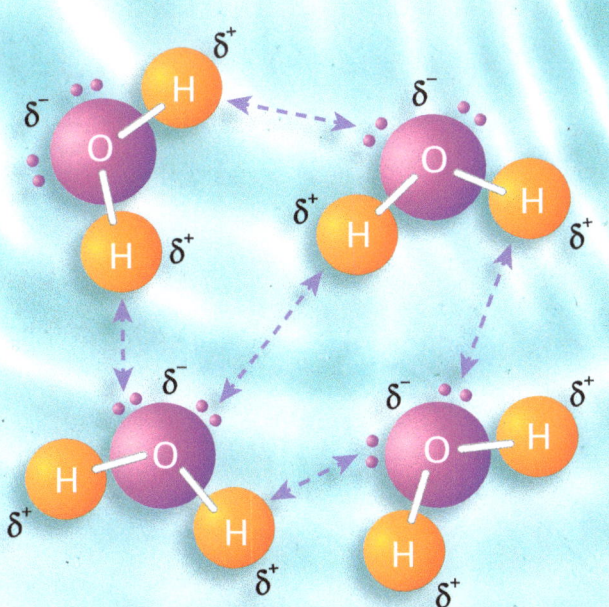

Water's polarity enables it to form a special kind of bond between molecules. The hydrogen atoms of one water molecule are attracted to the oxygen atom of another, producing an effect called *hydrogen bonding.*

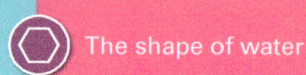
The shape of water

Surface tension

Surface tension enables objects to rest on the surface of water that would normally sink, such as needles, razor blades, and even certain insects!

DID YOU KNOW?

Scientists at the Chinese Academy of Sciences have found that water begins to form droplets with as little as five molecules!

I can feel the tension!

The water strider uses long, stiltlike legs to dart across the water's surface. It catches and eats other insects that fall into the water.

Hydrogen bonding gives water a special quirk—surface tension! Liquid water **molecules** on the surface of water form hydrogen bonds with one another, causing the surface to act like a thin, elastic film.

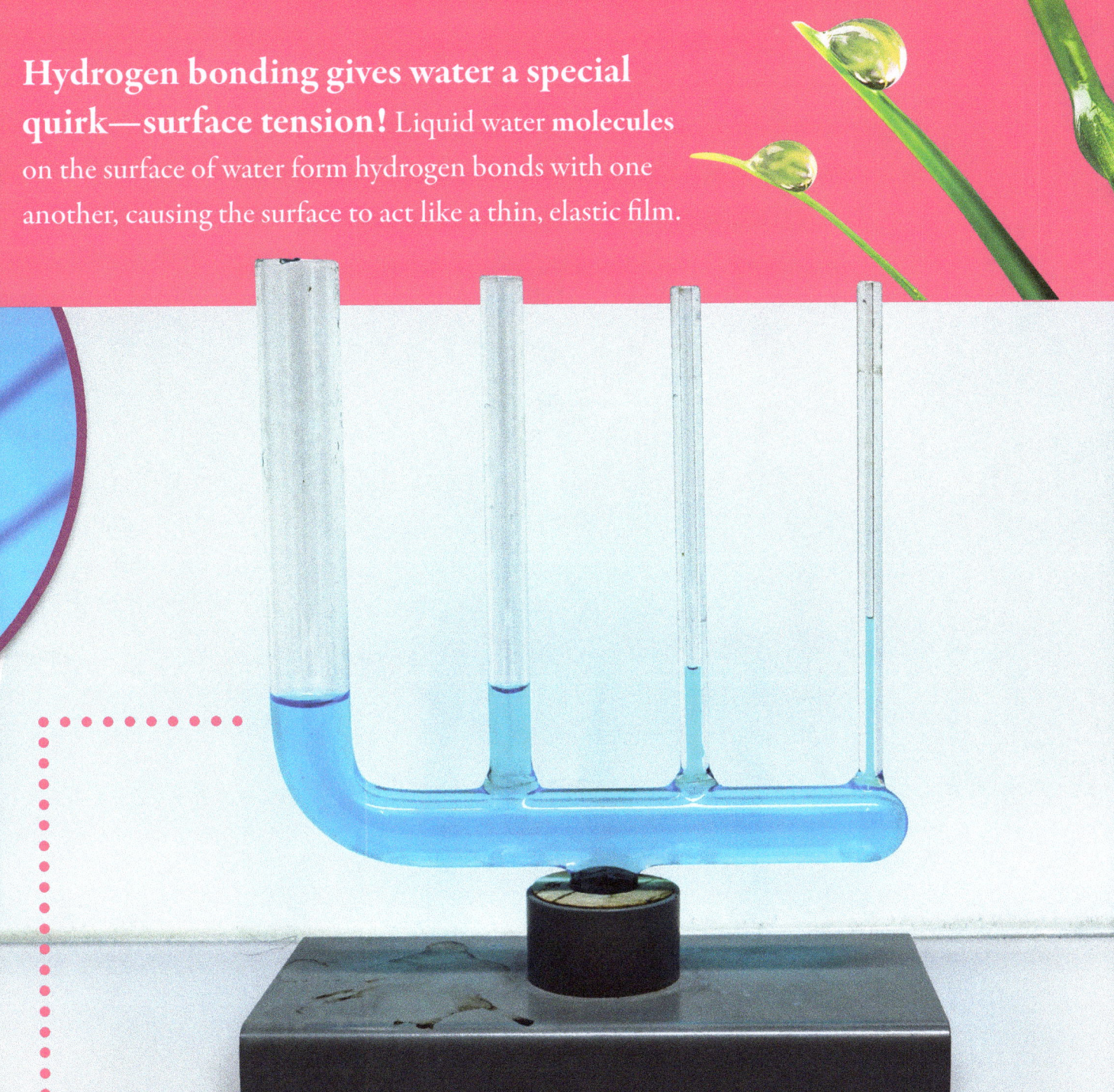

Hydrogen bonds* also enable water to climb** up tubes, against the force of gravity! This freaky ability is called ***capillary action. If the tube is narrow and its edges attract water, the water *molecules* around the edges are pulled upward. They, in turn, drag more molecules up through hydrogen bonds. If the tube is narrow enough, the water can rise several inches or centimeters!

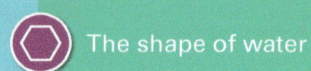 The shape of water

Electrolysis

In electrolysis, an electric current passes through a liquid, causing chemical reactions to occur.

When electricity is passed through water, it breaks apart water molecules. The atoms then form hydrogen gas (H_2) and oxygen gas (O_2).

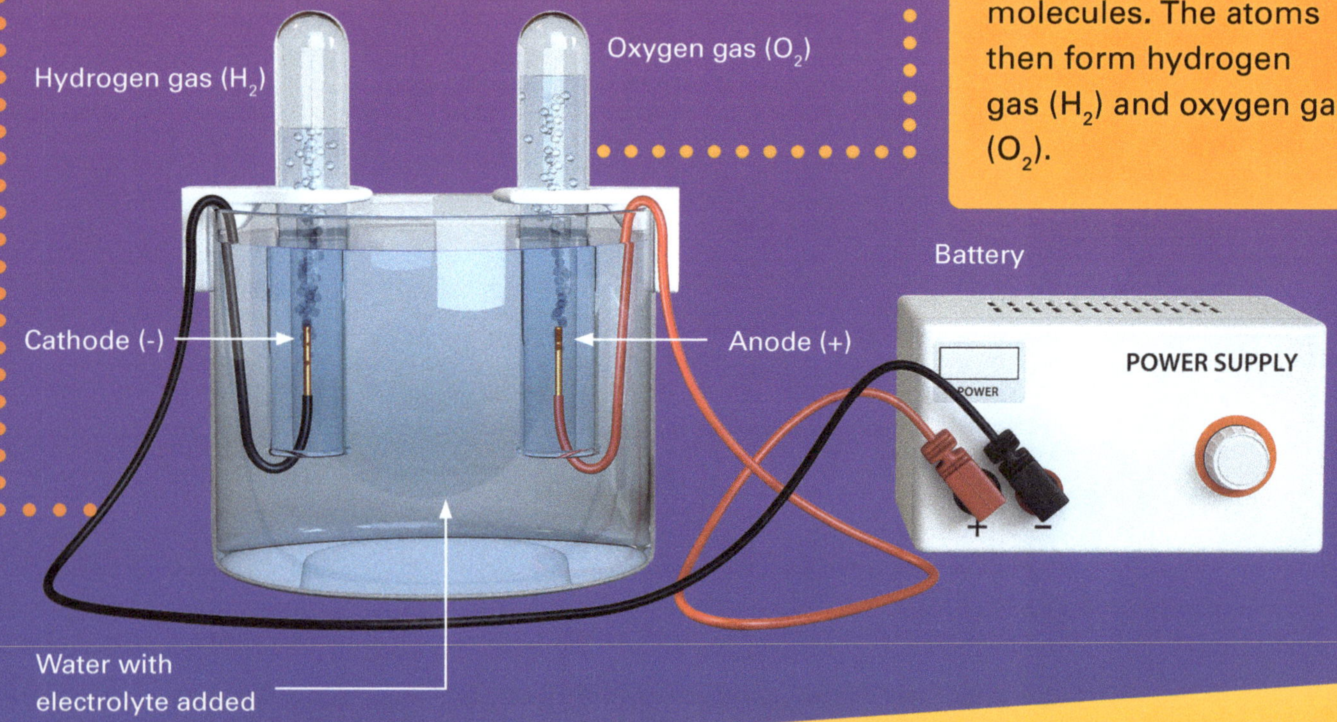

Hydrogen gas (H_2)

Oxygen gas (O_2)

Cathode (-)

Anode (+)

Battery

POWER SUPPLY

Water with electrolyte added

You might think that electrolysis would happen best with pure water. If you want the fastest reaction, use the purest ingredients, right? But, if you tried to electrolyze pure water, it wouldn't work at all! That's because pure water doesn't conduct electricity. You need other stuff in the water to conduct electric current.

12

Water is quite a stable *molecule*. It takes a lot of energy to break the bonds between the hydrogen and oxygen, but it's not impossible! It can be done through a process called **electrolysis**.

Electrolysis can also be used in a process called electroplating. In electroplating, metal ions are dissolved in water or another liquid, and an object made of a different metal is submerged in it. An electric current is applied to the object, causing the metal *ions* to attach to it. The object becomes plated with the new metal. This can make it more resistant to wear and rust or just make it look pretty!

TECH TIME

Think about it: If it takes lots of energy to split a water molecule, then forming one should make lots of energy. Inventors have developed fuel cells to put this energy to work. A fuel cell makes electrical energy from chemical energy by combining hydrogen and oxygen. Fuel cells could help reduce our dependence on fossil fuel-burning internal combustion engines. There are already fuel cell cars on the road! But, the technology is expensive, and there are few places to fill up with hydrogen.

Fill 'er up—with hydrogen!

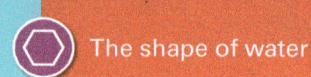 The shape of water

A soup of ions

An *ion* is an *atom* or *molecule* that has an electric charge. Atoms and molecules become charged if they gain or lose *electrons*. Ions can be held together in solids—think table salt!

Water, with its polar ends, is great at yanking apart ionic solids and dispersing the ions throughout the liquid. That means that almost every drop of water is full of ions and other minerals—like a bowl of ionic soup!

It's hard to find pure water in nature. The wet stuff almost always plays host to various impurities. One important class of impurities is ions.

Think about pouring table salt—also known as sodium chloride—into a glass of water. It seems to disappear! But if you drink the water, you can still taste the saltiness. The water broke apart the sodium chloride into sodium ions and chloride ions.

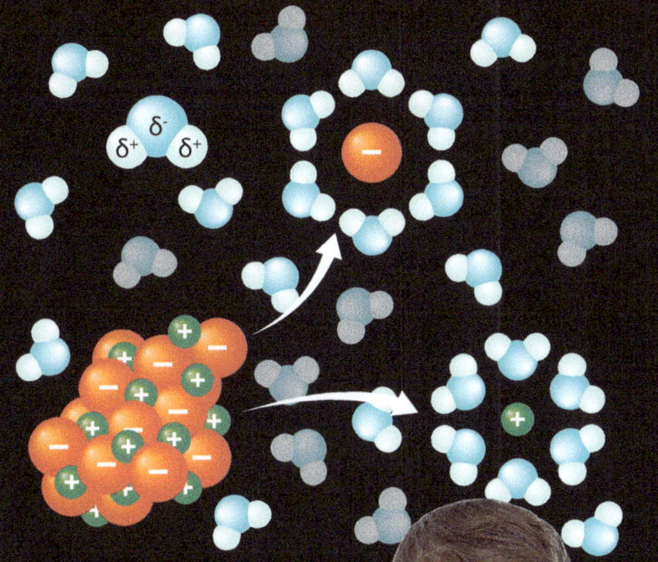

Molecules of liquid are always in motion—even in an apparently still glass of water. Once ions are dissolved, the natural movement of the water molecules spreads the ions through the water. This process is called diffusion. Think about that glass of salty water again. Each sip is salty.

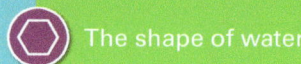
The shape of water

Desalination

Distillation is a desalting technique in which seawater is simply boiled and then condensed (returned to a liquid state). The ions don't boil, so the condensed vapor is pure H_2O.

Seawater is often desalted in desalination plants like this one.

TECH TIME

What do existing desalination techniques have in common? They're incredibly expensive! They use lots of energy, which costs lots of money. However, an engineering group based in China has developed a system that might turn that equation on its head. Using solar power to generate small currents, their device takes in water, evaporates some of it, and pushes the saltier stream back into the water supply. This technique helps to avoid the build-up of salts that can plague other systems. Its inventors claim that its solar-powered design and limited moving parts could enable it to desalt water more cheaply.

Things that have been dissolved in water aren't stuck there forever! And that's good, because people are using more fresh water than ever for drinking, growing crops, and manufacturing products. Scientists have developed ways to slake our serious thirst for pure water by removing the salt. This process is called **desalination,** or desalting.

Electrodialysis **involves a large chamber divided into many compartments** by stacks of two types of thin plastic membrane. One type allows only positive *ions* to pass through it. The other lets through only negative ions.

Two oppositely charged electrodes are placed at either end of the chamber. When an electric current is sent through the water, the negative ions are drawn through the membranes permeable to negative ions toward one of the electrodes. The positive ions are similarly drawn toward the other electrode.

Thus, the salt in every other compartment is drawn off, leaving fresh water.

Salt water

Concentrated brine

Fresh water

DID YOU KNOW?

The water in the world's oceans is so full of salt that it will make you sick if you drink it. Yuck!

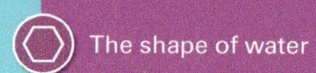
The shape of water

Water and cleaning

Remember how water is polar, with different parts having slightly different charges? Soap molecules have a positively charged head that is attracted to water. It's said to be hydrophilic. But, the molecule has a tail with no charge. This part, said to be hydrophobic, is repelled by water.

When put in water, soap molecules form bubbles. The tails attach to anything that isn't water—such as dirt and grime. Eventually, soap molecules encircle the dirt particle, and the water can carry it way.

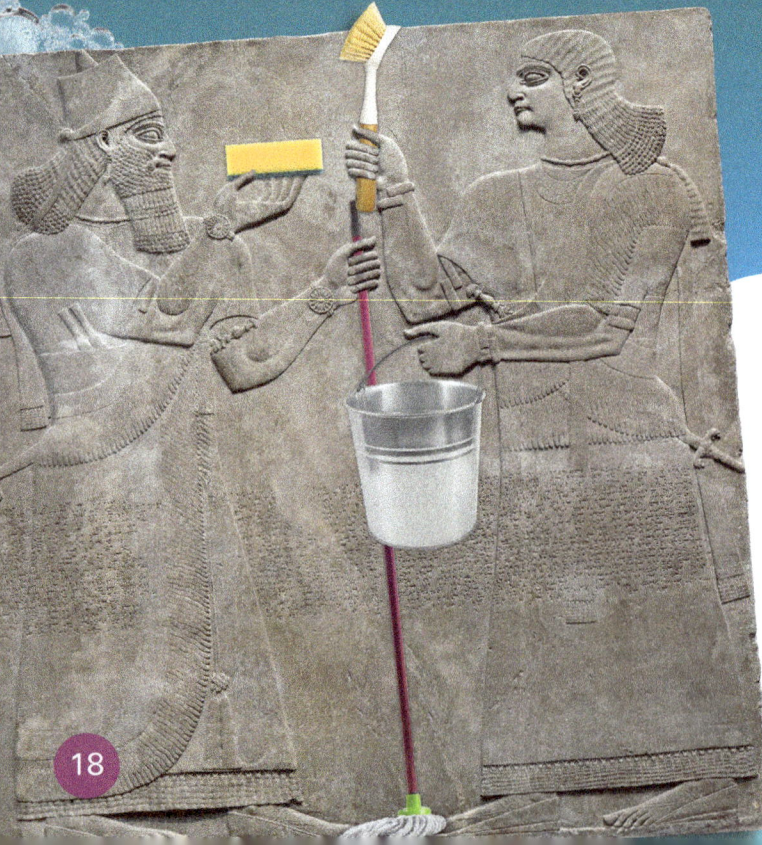

People have made soap for thousands of years using animal or plant fats. The **ancient Babylonians,** who lived in what is now Iraq, used soap almost 5,000 years ago!

Soaps and detergents can clean up messes that water alone can't. But, they need water's help to do the job!

Oil is water's archnemesis. Oils, fats, and grease are nonpolar. Each region of their molecules has the same charge. Therefore, water can't dissolve them well. You can see this in an oil-based salad dressing. The oil- and water-based parts separate out over a few minutes. Fortunately, soap can break up oils with water's help.

Because water is liquid at many temperatures on Earth and because of its polar molecules, it can dissolve many different materials. In fact, water is sometimes called the universal solvent because it can break down just about anything! Many stains can be scrubbed away with water alone!

② THE ELIXIR OF LIFE

Water is the elixir of life. Every living thing on Earth shares the need for water. Life on this planet is incredibly varied. Living things span the range from microbe to whale and mushroom to muskrat. They live in the upper atmosphere and at the bottom of the ocean. However, they all need water to survive.

A person can go about three weeks without food. But, a human being can only survive for about three days without water.

Water's properties enabled the first living things to form out of primitive soups of organic *molecules.* Life remained water-bound for billions of years. As living things moved onto land, obtaining and retaining water jumped to the top of their survival checklist.

SURVIVAL CHECKLIST
- Collect and save water
- Grow roots
- Grow leaves
- Thicken bark
- Reproduce

Water is vital to living things here on Earth, so scientists figure it must be important to alien life, if such life exists! Planets with surfaces capable of sustaining liquid water are thus said to be within their star's habitable zone. Other places scientists hope to find life include planets or moons with subsurface oceans.

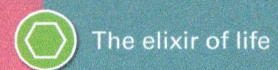

The elixir of life

Taking in water

Osmosis (Passive Transport)

Water is small enough to squeeze through the *molecules* of the cell membrane to get into and out of the cell. Ions and larger molecules are too large to pass in this way. This transfer is called *osmosis*, or passive transport.

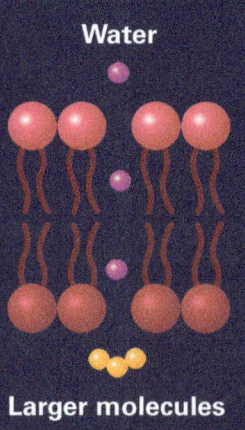

Aquaporins

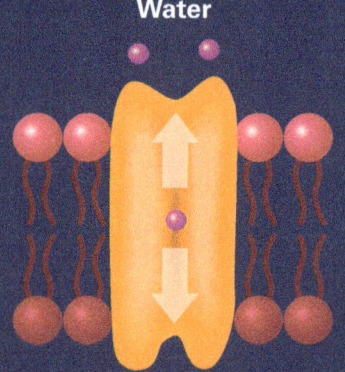

Sometimes, water needs to be moved into or out of the cell more quickly. Special pores in the cell membrane called *aquaporins* transport water in either direction—again leaving ions and larger molecules behind.

Reverse Osmosis

In osmosis, water usually moves from a lower concentration of dissolved substances toward a higher one. But what if you pressurize the salty side of the membrane? Higher pressure makes it harder for the water level to rise. At high enough pressure, the water molecules will start to accumulate on the other side of the membrane! This is called *reverse osmosis*, and it's another way to desalt water.

How does water get into cells? Do they all have tiny straws? Not exactly! Cells are enclosed by a special membrane. It is selectively permeable, meaning it can let some molecules in and keep others out.

The accolades came aquaporin in!

For years, we only knew half of the story of how water gets into and out of cells. American scientist **Peter Agre** discovered aquaporins in the mid-1990's. He shared the 2003 Nobel Prize in chemistry for his discovery.

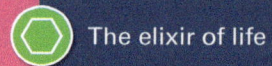
The elixir of life

Ocean chemistry

In 1872, the British chemist **Edward Sonstadt** reported on the existence of gold dissolved in seawater. Ever since, con-artist victims, dreamers, and even well-meaning scientists have been lured by the vast fortune just waiting to be unlocked. However, the tiny concentration of gold and the high cost of extracting it have thwarted every scheme.

CO_2

$CO_2 + H_2O \longrightarrow H^+ + HCO_2^-$
hydrogen ion — bicarbonate ion

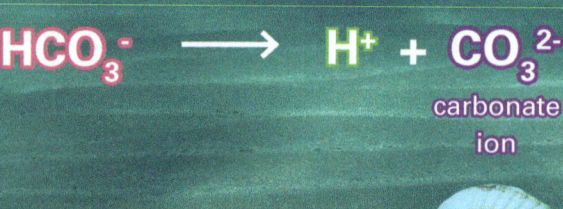
There's gold in them-there waves!

$HCO_3^- \longrightarrow H^+ + CO_3^{2-}$
carbonate ion

The ions present in seawater are vital for the living things there. The ions calcium and carbonate make up the shells and outer skeletons of many living things. A thin layer of living tissue absorbs these ions and deposits them on the growing edge of the shell to form calcium carbonate.

As we mentioned before, the ocean is full of ions. A glass of seawater is a veritable tour of the periodic table of elements.

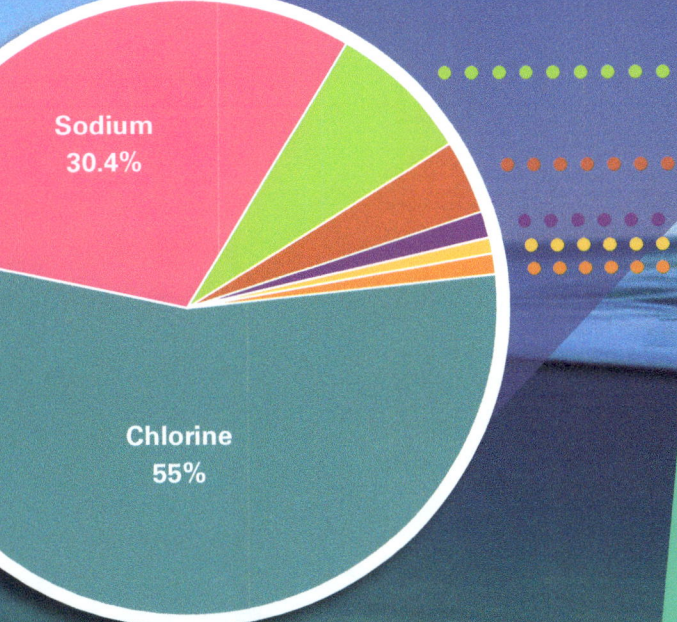

Water 96.5%

Dissolved salts 3.5%

Sodium 30.4%

Chlorine 55%

Sulfate (SO$_4$) 7.6%

Magnesium 3.9%

Calcium 1.2%

Potassium 1.1%

All other dissolved salt components >1%

You may have heard of lithium-ion batteries. They're the batteries found in almost every rechargeable electronic device—and now they're being used in electric cars, too! Unfortunately, lithium deposits are rare on Earth. But lithium can be found in the ocean. The concentrations are low but higher than that of gold. Several companies are developing technology to extract this lithium for use in batteries.

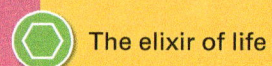
The elixir of life

Vital element: chlorine

STATS

Symbol
Cl

Atomic number
17

Atomic mass
35.453

Class
Halogens

- **The ionized form of chlorine,** called chloride, is not only harmless, but it's an essential part of living things. It's the lesser-known ingredient in table salt. But, when two chlorine atoms bond together, the product—chlorine gas—is deadly. It has many uses but must be handled with care.

The Swedish chemist **Carl Wilhelm Scheele** first made chlorine in 1774. In 1810, the English chemist Sir Humphry Davy determined that chlorine was a chemical element. He named it from a Greek word meaning greenish-yellow, after the coloration of the gas.

Gotcha!

No substance shows how variable chemicals can be better than chlorine. Depending on how it is bonded, it is either essential to living things or deadly.

Manufacturers produce chlorine gas chiefly by passing an electric current through solutions of sodium chloride. You could do it at home—but don't!

Whenever you take a dip in a sparkling swimming pool or take a sip of clean water, thank chlorine! Chlorine is widely used to purify drinking water and the water in swimming pools by killing any bacteria lurking there.

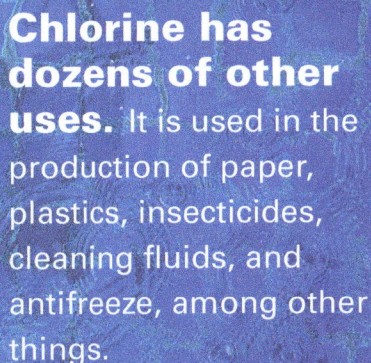

Chlorine has dozens of other uses. It is used in the production of paper, plastics, insecticides, cleaning fluids, and antifreeze, among other things.

3 DRINKING WATER

Water can feel hard when you belly-flop into a swimming pool, but that's not what we're talking about!

Water hardness refers to the concentration of dissolved calcium and magnesium ions. Hard water can leave stains and deposits, damage equipment, and make soap feel slimy.

You wouldn't want to drink from a dirty creek or lap up water from a mud puddle! Water is often purified so it is safe and tasty to drink.

Some people add special filters to their plumbing to reduce water hardness.

Impurities in tap water can cause long-term health problems. The most notorious example is the element lead (chemical symbol, Pb).

Hmm...needs more lead.

Until lead was found to be toxic, people used it for many purposes because it was abundant, easy to work, and resistant to rust. Lead pipes are still in use in some parts of the world. The **ancient Romans** even added lead salts to cheap wine to make it taste better! Yikes!

Drinking water

Tap water **taste**

Often, the compounds in water make it taste better! Various ions and minerals give water different tastes and textures.

Sodium chloride, of course, makes water taste salty.

Magnesium can make water taste sweet and gives it a crisp finish, but too much can make water taste bitter.

Too much calcium in water can leave your mouth feeling dry after you drink it.

Water may not be flavorful, but it does have a taste! The chemical compounds in tap water influence its taste.

Some compounds are never good for water flavor. One of these is the molecule hydrogen sulfide (H_2S). Produced by bacteria in plumbing or absorbed by boiling water in hot springs, H_2S imparts a characteristic "rotten egg" smell and taste to the water. Gross!

Some people think ultra-pure water may be unsafe to drink regularly. They think that without other dissolved compounds, too much of the water will flow into cells, stressing them out. Others say this claim is overblown. Whatever the case, ultra-pure water tastes weird! We're used to the taste of water with dissolved compounds and minerals in it.

CAREER CORNER

Can you taste the difference between tap water from two different places or two different kinds of bottled water? Maybe you could be a water sommelier! Water sommeliers test additive combinations to improve water flavor and mouthfeel for bottled water companies. They can even recommend water pairings to go with certain foods.

Drinking water

Fluoride in tap water

Fluoride is added to water to prevent tooth decay. Fluoride ions interfere with the production of acid by bacteria inside the mouth. This acid can damage teeth, so the fluoride helps to keep teeth healthy.

CAREER CORNER

It's vital to know what's in tap water. Water quality technicians help us find out! They test tap water, as well as water from rivers, lakes, or the ocean, to monitor chemical levels and check for contaminants.

Glowing green…not a good sign.

Some additives to tap water improve not taste, but health.
One such substance is the ion fluoride.

Don't swallow your toothpaste! Many toothpastes have fluoride to prevent tooth decay. If you swallow a little toothpaste, you probably won't get sick. But swallowing too much flouride can actually damage the appearance of the teeth, staining them.

Smile!

Would you be happy with brown-stained teeth if it meant you would never get cavities? In 1901, the dentist **Frederick McKay** observed that many children in Colorado Springs, Colorado, had permanent brown stains on their teeth. But, the stained teeth were resistant to tooth decay. Quite the tradeoff! In 1931, McKay and others discovered that the town's water supply had high levels of fluoride. Later research showed that a small amount of fluoride could protect against tooth decay—without producing unsightly stains.

4 DIRTY WATER

Sewage is water that contains waste matter produced by human beings. This dirty water is a huge problem. It can make people sick and harm the environment, so it must be treated before it is returned to lakes and streams.

What happens to all the water that goes down the drain or gets flushed down the toilet? It becomes wastewater.

Sewage is not the only way water gets dirty. Rainwater mixes with pollutants and transports them hither and yon, sometimes into sewage systems or into other parts of the environment. Carbon dioxide emissions from the combustion of fossil fuels can seep into lakes and oceans, upsetting the chemistry of water.

DID YOU KNOW?

In the United States alone, households produce some 30 billion gallons (125 billion liters) of wastewater per day!

Dirty water

Water damage

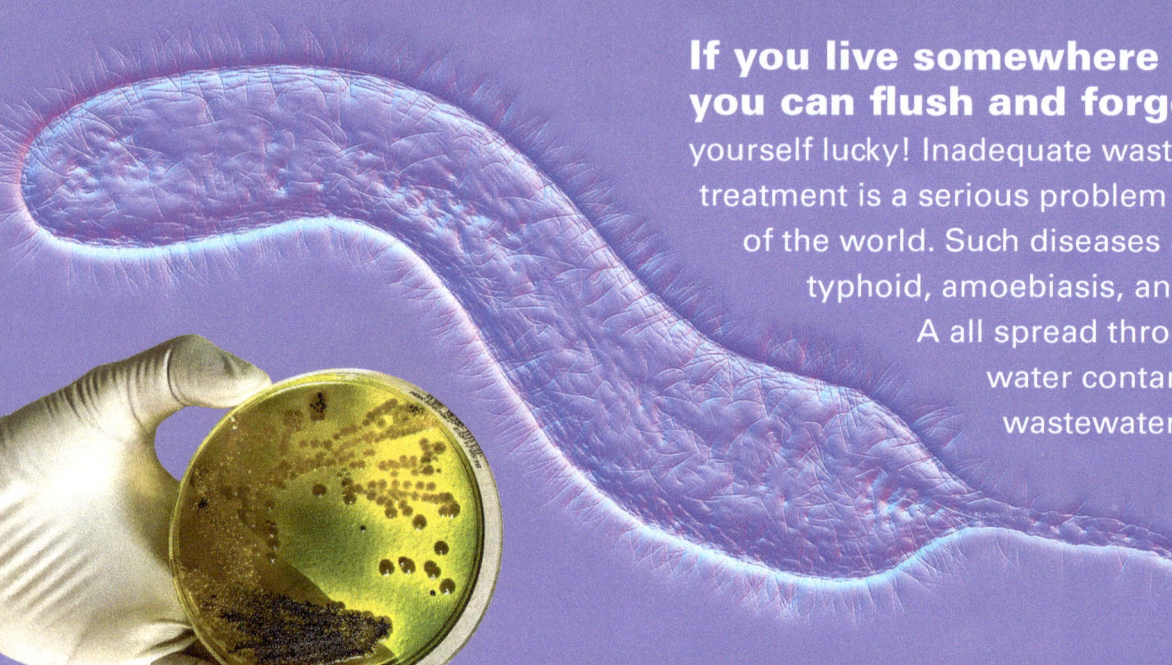

If you live somewhere where you can flush and forget, consider yourself lucky! Inadequate wastewater treatment is a serious problem in many parts of the world. Such diseases as cholera, typhoid, amoebiasis, and hepatitis A all spread through drinking water contaminated with wastewater.

CURIOUS CONNECTIONS

ENGINEERING An ounce of prevention is worth a pound of cure! Fertilizer runoff is a major source of water pollution. An American company is designing a robot called Rowbot that could lessen such pollution by reducing the amount of fertilizer used. Rowbot is narrow enough to trundle between rows of corn. Using machine learning, it will identify the base of each corn plant and spray a small amount of fertilizer near it.

Sewage and other polluted water should be treated before it enters the environment, but that does not always happen. The result can be severe illness in people and damage to the environment.

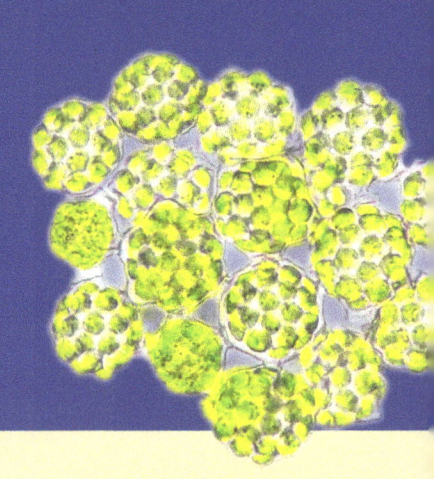

Eutrophication is a water pollution problem caused by runoff from fertilizer.
Natural water environments maintain a delicate balance between nutrients and the living things that feed on them. Fertilizer runoff can supercharge the water with nutrients, fueling blooms of tiny living things called algae.

I like algae, but this is ri-duck-ulous!

What's wrong with a little extra algae?
Algae are photosynthetic, which means they need light from the sun to survive. As they reproduce rapidly in the runoff-polluted water, the algae in deeper waters dies because algae near the surface block out the light. The decomposing algae suck oxygen out of the water. With too little oxygen in the water, fish and other larger animals begin to die, kicking off a runaway cycle. Eventually, the water has too little oxygen to support any life.

 Dirty water

Ocean acidification

Before

After

Living things in the ocean build their shells from calcium and carbonate ions in the oceans. Those carbonate *ions* form as carbon dioxide dissolves into seawater.

$$CO_2 + H_2O \rightleftharpoons CO_3^{2-} + 2H^+$$

The hydrogen ions released in this reaction make the water slightly acidic. The increase of such ions in the water is called ocean acidification.

Warmer temperatures and more acidic water can contribute to a damaging problem called coral bleaching.

Excess carbon dioxide released into the atmosphere isn't just an air problem. Everything in the natural world is connected. The greenhouse gas can harm ocean life, too.

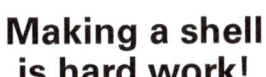

Making a shell is hard work!

Excess carbon dioxide makes it harder for living things to form shells. As the shell-building tissues of living things in the ocean deposit calcium carbonate, they expend energy to pump hydrogen ions back into the water. Otherwise, the carbonate shells can't form. When there's more carbon dioxide in the atmosphere, there are more carbonate and hydrogen ions in the water. Shell builders must expend more energy to build their shells. That's less energy that they can use to survive and reproduce.

CAREER CORNER

Want to study ocean acidification and its effect on sea life? Become an oceanographer! Oceanographers are scientists who study the sea floor, seawater, and sea life. They may specialize in biology, chemistry, engineering, geology, or physics.

Dirty water

Wastewater treatment

Wastewater treatment is a complex process that involves removing all excess solids and putting the water through a multistep filtration process. Only then is the water released into a local lake, stream, or wetland, where natural processes can continue to clean the water.

Most municipalities don't just dump their sewage into the environment. They treat it first!

In places not served by public sewers, most homeowners use septic tanks to treat their sewage. Sewage flows into a concrete or steel container buried underground. Solids in the sewage sink to the bottom of the tank or float to the surface. Bacteria in the sewage digest the solids.

This digestion process changes most of the wastes into gas and a harmless substance called humus. The gas escapes into the air. The humus in the tank must be pumped out periodically and taken to a sewage treatment plant.

 Dirty water

Treatment alternatives

Not all water used in a home is extremely dirty. And, not all water needs to be perfectly clean. Some homes make use of gray water systems. Gray water is any used water that hasn't been mixed with human waste. Gray water can be used to flush toilets, for example. If the homeowners use the right kind of soaps and detergents, gray water can even be used to water gardens!

Human feces (solid wastes) are full of pathogens, but they're also full of nutrients! Special toilets exist that turn this toxic sludge into harmless—even helpful—fertilizer! Such composting toilets need no water supply, making them ideal for rural settings.

Wastewater treatment and septic facilities are essential parts of cleaning the water where they are installed. But, it takes lots of money and resources to set them up and keep them running. Many inventors think it's time for a reevaluation of our wastewater systems.

TECH TIME

Urine wasn't always thought of as useless waste. In fact, it was collected and used for industrial processes for many years. It was even taxed! Urine-diverting (UD) toilets are designed to catch urine for other uses, keeping it out of the main wastewater stream. This urine could be collected and used for industrial purposes—just like the good old days!

Make a solar still

You will need:
- Plastic wrap
- Large bowl
- Salt
- Small rock or other weight
- Small glass cup or bowl
- Spoon
- Water

Give it a try

1. First, make your salt water. Pour about 1 inch or a few centimeters of water into the large bowl. Add plenty of salt and stir it up. Take a small taste to see how salty it is. Yuck!
2. Now, place the cup in the center of the bowl.
3. Loosely cover the bowl with a layer of plastic wrap.
4. Place a small rock in the middle of the plastic wrap, directly over the glass cup.
5. Place the solar still outdoors in an area with full sunlight.
6. In a couple of hours, some salt-free water should collect in your glass. Open up your still and take a sip!

Clean water is essential to living things—including us! In this experiment, you can purify water using only the power of the sun. It's a bright idea!

Try this next!

Experiment with different designs. Try a different bowl material or a deeper or shallower curve to the plastic wrap. Try adding food coloring to the water to see if the solar still filters it out. See if you can collect clean water from fresh leaves. (Don't taste the distilled product, though!).

QUESTION TIME!

Do you think a solar still is a good method of purifying water? Why or why not? Where could it be useful? Where are other water purification methods more practical?

Index

A
Agre, Peter, 23
algae, 37
aquaporins, 22-23
atoms, 7-9, 12, 14, 26

B
Babylon, ancient, 18
bacteria, 27, 31-32, 41

C
calcium, 24-25, 28, 30, 38
calcium carbonate, 24, 39
capillary action, 11
carbon dioxide, 35, 38-39
carbonate, 24, 38-39
cells, 22-23, 31
Celsius, Anders, 9
Chinese Academy of Sciences, 10
chloride, 15, 26
chlorine, 25-27
coral bleaching, 38
covalent bonds, 8

D
Davy, Sir Humphry, 26
dental health, 32-33
desalination, 16-17, 22
diffusion, 15
distillation, 16, 44-45

E
electricity, 12-13, 27
electrodialysis, 17
electrolysis, 12-13
electrons, 7-8, 14
electroplating, 13
eutrophication, 37

F
fertilizer, 36-37, 42
fluoride, 32-33
fuel cells, 13

G
gold, 24
gray water, 42
Greece, ancient, 7

H
habitable zones, 21
hard water, 28
hydrogen, 7-9, 11-13, 24, 38-39
hydrogen bonding, 9, 11
hydrogen sulfide, 31

I
ions, 13-16, 22, 24-25, 28, 30, 32-33, 38-39

L
lead, 29

46

lithium-ion batteries, 25

M
magnesium, 25, 28, 30
McKay, Frederick, 33
molecules, 6-15, 18-19, 21-23, 31

N
neutrons, 7

O
ocean acidification, 38-39
oceanography (career), 39
oils, 19
osmosis, 22
oxygen, 7-9, 12-13, 37

P
potassium, 25
protons, 7

R
reverse osmosis, 22
Rome, ancient, 29
Rowbot (robot), 36

S
salt, 14-17, 22, 26-27, 30, 44
Scheele, Carl Wilhelm, 26
sewage, 34-37, 40-41

shells, 24, 38-39
soap, 18-19, 28, 42
sodium, 15, 25
sodium chloride. *See* salt
solar power, 16
solar stills, 44-45
Sonstadt, Edward, 24
sulfate, 25
surface tension, 10-11

T
tap water, 29-33

U
urine-diverting (UD) toilets, 43

W
wastewater, 34-37, 40-43
water quality technician (career), 32
water sommelier (career), 31
water striders, 10
water treatment, 40-43

Glossary

aquaporin (ak wuh PAWR uhn)—a protein in the cell membrane that admits large numbers of water molecules but blocks other molecules, even those that resemble water

atom (AT uhm)—one of the most basic units of matter, consisting of a nucleus (core) of particles called protons and neutrons with tiny particles called electrons moving around the nucleus

capillary action (KAP uh LEHR ee AK shuhn)—the tendency of liquids to move into or out of tiny, hairlike passageways. The action depends on surface tension—that is, the attraction of the molecules at a liquid's surface for each other.

covalent bond (koh VAY luhnt bond)—a chemical bond between atoms where each of two atoms contributes one electron to a pair, which the atoms then share

desalination (dee SAL uh NAY shuhn)—also known as desalting, the process of removing salt from seawater or other salty water

distillation (DIHS tuh LAY shuhn)—a method of desalination by which salty water is boiled and the steam is collected

electrodialysis (ih LEHK troh dy AL uh sihs)—a method of desalination by which an electric current is sent through salty water in a chamber with stacks of thin membranes

electrolysis (ih LEHK TROL uh sihs)—the use if electric current to separate chemical elements

electron (ih LEHK tron)—a tiny particle with no charge that moves around the nucleus of an atom

hydrogen bonding (HY druh john BON dihng)—a weak intermolecular attraction between a hydrogen atom in one molecule and an electron pair associated with an oxygen, nitrogen, or fluorine atom in another molecule

ion (EYE uhn)—an atom or molecule that has an electric charge

molecule (MOL uh kyool)—two or more atoms bonded together

neutron (NOO tron)—a tiny particle with no charge that, together with protons, form the nuclei of almost all atoms

osmosis (oz MOH sihs)—the movement of liquid from one solution through a special membrane into a more concentrated solution

proton (PROH ton)—a tiny particle with a positive charge that is found in the nucleus of an atom.

reverse osmosis (rih VURS oz MOH sihs)—a method of desalination by which pressure is applied to salty water, forcing the water through a salt-filtering membrane

www.ingramcontent.com/pod-product-compliance
Lightning Source LLC
Chambersburg PA
CBHW061250170426
43191CB00041B/2409